Sis, Be the Bag

Written by: *Lashonda Mchenry*

Copyrights @ 2020 Investments 4ever, LLC.

All rights reserved

ISBN: 9798644817474

Thank you for making the choice of being a part of "I Am the BAG" Academy. I will be your Coach. By the end of this academy, you will look at your life in a totally different way.

INTRODUCTION

My life has not always been peaches and cream. I had to go through many experiences to get where I am today. The journey of being young and dumb to mature and being wise, definitely did not happen overnight. We all must find ourselves at some point of our lives. We all must go through trial and error while learning who we are.

Either you go through the fire with the courage of not getting burned or you stay watching the fire get larger while debating on going through. You must go through some things to have a story to tell. I stress this with every breathe in me. You must be able to accept and embrace who you are and not who you pretend to be to the world. Some of us live in this imaginary life for so long to the point we start to believe the lie we created. I am guilty of this myself. Stop trying to please people that do not give a damn about you.

I am very transparent with my life. I am not afraid to share my good & bad moments with the world. I know my purpose on earth is to change the lives of others. I accept my assignment. The hype of the good life can lure you right in. You can get caught up in the cyber world of make believe. You can get caught up in the illusion of lives you see from the outside because you do not know their real story. You do not witness the prettiest chicks on social media crying and stressing. You only see what they post and who they seem to be. You now begin to wish this life for yourself. You begin to lust for it. Your soul begins to crave the glamourous life. You want the Gucci, Chanel, and all the other name brands. We all want to be able to wear a pair of Red Bottoms. Some can transition very easily into that world and some can easily get lost. It is all in your mindset. Is your mental state of mind strong?

I never tried any drugs besides marijuana years ago. I use to hear stories about real drug addicts and things they will do for a high. I have witnessed crackheads go through withdrawals because they cannot get their drugs. I guess I shared a common sickness as a drug addict or crackhead. I had a high for money & all the glitz and glamour that came with it. I was a fiend for the life I wanted. I became a risk taker more than anyone I hung around.

There are two types of people in this world. Those that make it happen and those that watch it happen. Guess which one I am? Understand it is okay to copy a cat if it is the right cat you copy. Nobody wants to lose or be considered a loser. Even those that watch from the sideline. Many people must face that word defeat to become humble and levelheaded. I am blessed to be on my own winning team now. I am blessed to be alive. I am blessed to be free. I am blessed to be able to talk to you and encourage you to be the bag.

Sis, we do not chase a bag. We chase our passion. We are the BAG!!

- Beautiful and Godly
- Bosses Accept God
- Bosses and Grinding
- Bosses Achieving Goals
- Billionaires Always Getting It

The BAG stands for many things. You stand for those things. You are now a part of this movement. A movement to empower and inspire your sisters.

Again, I welcome to "I Am the BAG" Academy....

My DNA of being a Hustler runs deep. Giving up has never been an option for me. And will not be an option for you. If you think about giving up, reprogram your thoughts, and strengthen your mindset. Everything forms in the brain. Determination plays a key role in being successful. Sis always be determined.

Allow me to take you on this journey of life lessons and knowledge. These tips will take you a long way in your own life!! Use each gem as a key to unlock all your desires. You can now call me Coach *Shon*.

Before we go into our lessons, I want you to repeat these words and mean it. Take a deep breath and say it from the bottom of your gut. Repeat it until you believe it. Repeat it until you manifest it.

- I AM A QUEEN
- I AM BLESSED
- I AM THE BAG
- I WILL NEVER ACCEPT LESS THAN WHAT I DESERVE
- I WILL NEVER ALLOW PEOPLE TO DISTRACT ME FROM MY VISION
- I AM BEAUTIFUL
- I AM A BOSS
- I AM LOVED AND I GIVE LOVE
- I AM (say your entire name)

It is never too late to start over and elevate to another level in life. Everybody did not become a wealthy individual overnight. Everything takes time and patience. You must believe in yourself. You must invest in yourself. Plant your own seeds first and ask God to bless it. Then watch it grow!

I had some amazing ladies to share some words of encouragement with you. Each one of these ladies hold a special place in my heart and I cherish their advice. I decided to share these ladies with you.

"Ladies fully love yourself. Always focus on what is important: Yourself and your goals."

-Rasheda Byrd

"Ladies, make a plan, set goals, do not be afraid and take risks. That's your success."

-Desiree Nugent

"Ladies invest in yourself. There is always something to learn, you can never learn too much. Never stop chasing your dreams. You may fall but the win comes when you get up."

-Karen Cooper

"Ladies believe and trust in yourself. Embrace failures because you truly never fail. You learn what NOT to do the next time. Create your own path; every road to success looks different!"

-Latavia Banks

"Ladies you are the true definition of a hustler! Keep your momentum and your stride. The people along your journey will learn valuable lessons."

-Alecia Baker

Always align yourself with people who can guide you and teach you. Never base relationships on years. Base relationships on how it affects your life. Is the relationship beneficial or artificial? You decide.

CHAPTERS OF KNOWLEDGE

- Discover Who You Are
- Identify Your Gifts & Talents
- Credit & Saving Money
- Set Goals
- Speak Life into Yourself Everyday
- Mental Love Is the Strongest Love
- Essential Business Owner or Essential Career
- Brand and Market Yourself
- Protect Your Peace
- Who Are You Aligned With?
- Make Smart Investments
- Passion Attracts Blessings & Money
- Defeat the Odds
- Secure the Vault
- High Frequency of Energy: Law of Attraction

DISCOVER WHO YOU ARE

First allow me to give praise to the high. Prayers are powerful and you hold all the power in your thoughts. Always feed yourself positive thoughts. Never be afraid to correct those around you that display negative vibes. Those spirits are transferrable. Learn to change a negative conversation into a positive one. It is all in your mindset. You must always protect your peace. Sis do not be afraid to reset your mind. If you know you can be negative, feed yourself great thoughts. You need to speak positive words. You need to act in positive ways. You must be an example of great leadership. Do not be afraid to put yourself in uncomfortable situations. When we accept being complacent, we will not elevate to the next level. GET UNCOMFORTABLE!

My journey of becoming wise took time. Let me just say many years. I wish I knew then what I know now. But if I did, I would not be able to share this with you. I had to go through some things to understand the importance of life. I had to discover who I was and who God created me to be. I am changing every day. You are changing every day. Never allow people to define who you are especially when they do not know themselves. Never allow others to dictate your limitations.

At an early age I got caught up in the fast life. I wanted all the money. I craved for all the money. So, I learned many ways to get the money. It was never enough for me. I was chasing the money. I was chasing the bag. Sis never chase the BAG. For so many years, the money was running away from me because anything you chase is going in the opposite direction. I was chasing the money with no passion in the mist of it. The root of evil is not money. It is the love for the money and what you will do to get it. I realized I was loving the wrong thing. I was putting too much energy into the world of things that held no value. I had to have love for my passions first. Now I know to focus my energy on my desires, my passions, and my visions. I will always be a magnet to attract the money and all the success aligned with it.

Things I did, I did not have to do. This is what makes my life so unique. I was born into a family of well-established people. Some were hard workers in the career field and some were self-employed. Both were financially stable. Growing up I did a lot of wrong things or should I say experienced things because of curiosity. Yes, curiosity kills the cat but it will never kill the right cat. I made many dumb decisions. I took many dumb risks. Things I chose to take part in, people I chose to associate myself with; could have landed me in prison or dead. Thank God, he looks after babies and fools. I could have thrown my entire life away because of my immature thinking at the time. I was trying to be a part of something I thought was great. A part of something I thought was cool.

One day it hit me. All the money I was coming into. All the rich people I was building relationships with; meant nothing if you had nothing to show for it. I was running through money as fast as I got it. I was around millionaires like I was one. It was all a dream (in my Biggie voice). I was in a fairy tale world. A world I believed was true. I got lost and drowned in this fantasy of other people lives. My money moves were not essential. When there was a drought, nothing moved and no money was being made. I had only learned how to get money when the streets were moving. What happens when it stops? What other options did I have? Could I survive when the streets stop?

As I began to mature and got tired of going through the recess periods of no money. I had to think on a creative mindset. I had to think outside the box. You know there is a big world outside of that box you keep your mind captive in. You may never experience being locked up in jail or prison physically but mentally you been in prison for years. You only think one way. You only believe one thing. You will not allow your mind to think beyond what you can see with your eyes. Let your brain free itself!! Walk by faith not by site is a real statement. Do you walk by faith? Do you walk by site? I learned my belief is bigger than what I saw. I began to manifest everything I desired.

I had to put on my big girl panties and find a better way. But first I had to go through the embarrassment stage of becoming humble. I had to be embarrassed of myself. I was not embarrassed to the world because the world never knew what I was going through. You never let the outside destroy you before you build yourself up. You must learn to be transparent with yourself. Point out all your flaws and embrace them. Identify what you need to work on. Never allow the world to pinpoint your weakness because they will use it against you. If you already know who you are. The words or thoughts of others and how they feel about you; will never matter. The mind is a muscle. The more you train it and work it out, the stronger it becomes. God had to strip me of everything for me to appreciate my strongest power, My mind!

My homeboys named me, Pooh Gotti. I was a female rapper out of Miami, Florida. I grew up in Opa Locka. I was very known to many in the music industry. I held a huge reputation of holding my own in an industry dominated by males. I was a little thug, but I was sexy with it. I earned the name Pooh Gotti.

Pooh Gotti embraced the fast life in a whole separate way. She attracted the millionaires. She attracted the fast life on a whole different level. Pooh Gotti swallowed Lashonda whole. Lashonda did not have a chance to shine in the same light as Pooh Gotti during that time. When I finally realized what happened to me. I had a lot of self-searching to do. I had to find me again if I wanted to receive all my blessings. Remember God cannot bless the fake you.

Let me tell you how God sat me down and made me figure out where I was at this point. Pooh Gotti had 2 distribution deals on the table. These distribution deals were not offered at the same time. Every time I got close to signing a distribution deal, something always went wrong with the companies I was signed with. I am a spiritual person. I grew up in a praying family. I sat back and prayed. I could not understand why this kept happening to me. I finally realized a few things.

Mistake 1:

- Not knowing who I was. Not knowing who God created me to be. I needed Lashonda. I needed to know Lashonda.

Mistake 2:

- I was not aligned with the right individuals. I always said when I make it, I was going to take care of everyone. Everyone is not meant to share in your journey of blessings. If you have people around you and you know they not right. God will delay your blessings until you follow his directives to remove them.

I understood at that moment that the situations that took place with my record companies, was about me. Not the actual people it was happening to.

God will not bless mess and I was a whole mess. I needed to mentally clean myself up. It is time to separate, evaluate, and elevate. First, I had to complete these steps within myself. It was time for the faceoff; Lashonda vs Pooh Gotti. I had to get Lashonda's power back. I had to re-introduce Lashonda to Pooh Gotti. I had to build a bond with her and fall in love with her all over again because we were so disconnected. Lashonda is humble. Lashonda does not care about material things. Lashonda does not care if a man is rich. She will love him just for being a real MAN. Lashonda was so different from Pooh Gotti. Lashonda enjoys the rich life but she gravitates to the knowledge of how they became rich. She wants to learn and strategize a blueprint. Pooh Gotti does not care how they became rich. She only cared about the life it brought into hers. Pooh Gotti loved popping bottles and VIP treatment. Lashonda appreciates the moments of popping bottles and VIP treatment. These two ladies love a lot of the same things but appreciate them in two different ways.

I had to learn me all over again. It was like teaching a baby how to walk. But I did just that. I took so much time with myself. I went everywhere by myself. I went out to eat by myself. I learned to embrace my own company. I realized I had forgotten about the world around me. Now I am disconnected to what is going on. I no longer craved the streets the way I use to. I no longer craved the nightlife like I use to. I no longer wanted the fast money. I wanted financial stability. I no longer wanted the "got to make it happen" schemes. Lashonda manifested abundance and peace. Lashonda embrace knowledge and positivity. Lashonda is focused on her passion to be blessed in every way placed along her journey. Lashonda prays for a certain type of man. She does not care to have a grown boy. Lashonda will not lower her standards of a man just to have one. Lashonda's mindset is totally different now. I stepped into the woman I lost so many years ago. I finally embraced all of her.

Remember, everyone will not change when you do. Everyone will not accept your change. Please do not expect them to. It is only for your understanding. This will expose those who should be cut off. Do not be afraid to let go. It could be your husband. It could be your best friend. It could be your cousin. Do what you need to do to become a better you.

I graduated from high school with my Diploma. I have a degree in Psychology. I am a Notary Agent. I am a licensed Braider. I am a Certified Tax Preparer. I am an Author. I am a Writer. I am a Leadership Coach to many people. I am a Truth speaker. I have so many other things I want to do and will accomplish. This is only the beginning. Lashonda knows who she is and what she wants. She did not come to play. It is strictly business with her. Pooh Gotti had to take a step back and let Lashonda lead the way from this point on. Eventually, Lashonda began to teach Pooh Gotti some things. It all worked out for the great. Teamwork makes the dream work. Embrace everything about yourself even the many personalities. Identify your personalities. You are not crazy. These personalities make you who you are. You must know the order of which they fall.

IDENTIFY YOUR GIFTS & TALENTS

Figure out what you can do. What you love doing? It could be cooking, doing hair, designing clothes, singing, rapping, writing, bartending, dancing, etc... Find your gifts. God blessed you with powers when he created you. Your powers are your gifts and talents. Those are the things you were blessed with. They will get you through your journey of life. God already know what he embedded in you. It is your job to know who you are and identify your many blessings.

Did you watch cartoons as a kid? Pay attention to the cartoons. Every character had superpowers or something special about them. That is how you are equipped too. You have superpowers that you have to activate within yourself.

I always knew I would be into the music industry because at a young age I danced and sang. Later I discovered my writing skills. I began to write poetry. I turned my poems into lyrics. I started doing hair at the age of 6. It made me grow a passion for being creative in the hair business. I loved doing hair. I started doing everybody hair. I taught myself how to braid hair. Knowing how to braid hair put me in a great position.

Discovering your gifts and talents is a must. I could dance, sing, braid hair, and get in the minds of others. When I started making money from doing hair at the age of 10, I became a beast. I was actually getting paid to braid and create styles for my clients. I provided a service that gave me income. I learned how to handle business early.

I remember my family would put me in every dance contest. I would win every time. Most of the contests rewarded me with money. Plus, my family would bless me with money. They were my biggest cheerleaders. Do you have a great support system? Identify those who always have your back no matter what. Not just financially but mentally and spiritually. Those are the ones you keep close.

When I became a teenager. The love of money grew even bigger. I had a steady clientele for hair. I was learning the street game at the same time. My boys were teaching me the ropes. I learned how to take my hair money and flip it in the streets. Every other day I watched my money double and triple in return. This created a monster in me.

I started meeting dudes who were into streets heavy. It matched my mentally at that time. I wanted my hands in everything every opportunity I was presented with. Again, I used my gifts and talents to make me money.

Use your gifts and talents to make you money. Allow it to create the life you desire. This is the purpose of identifying who you are and what you are equipped with. You know a girl name Kim. Kim cooks dinners everyday and make great money. You decide to cook dinners too. You do not make as much money as Kim. Do you know why? Kim is a cook. Cooking is Kim's passion. You are not a cook. You just wanted to make money. You design clothes. Stick to your gift.

When I started rapping, I began to hang around stars. I hung around celebrities I watched on television. I never built my relationships with them off music. My relationships were built through me braiding their hair. Oh, and I am real smart. I never wanted them to know I rapped. I just wanted to be the braider.

Hanging around guys all day and everyday had its pros. I learned the game from a male prospective. Most of all

I learned how to finesse a guy when it came to him liking me. I learned how to manipulate the minds of many people with my finesse. This is when I discovered how to get into a dude's head. Once I mastered this technique, it was on and popping. Crazy part about that was I did not know nothing about Psychology. This gift was embedded in me.

Now I am known for braiding the hair of celebrities. My clientele grew bigger and the money was increasing on a steady pace. I am flipping my coins rapidly in these drug infested streets. I am rapping and getting paid shows. I had a Manager on point. I am dealing with dudes who got plenty of money and was not hesitating to spend it. I was the ideal female for many dudes. I used my image at my advantage. Remember, people believe only what you show them. You believe the life of that celebrity because you see it with your eyes. Perception is everything in the world we live in. What is the perception of your life to others? Is it a good image? Do you need to work on it? Only you can rebrand who you are. Only you can show the world who you are. Set the tone of your life. Do not let anyone set it for you.

At this point I should have been good and focused. But I wanted more. I decided to become a stripper. Yes, I wanted to experience that life too. I wanted to see what the hype was all about. I did not want to dance in a rachet club. Plus, I had a white girl shape and I loved it. When I danced, females were not into getting their bodies done. It was only the rich people into that. I decided to dance in a Spanish club. I made a lot of money in there. I made a lot of connections in there. I built many relationships in there. I learned about another world in there.

So, I hope you following me? Gifts and Talents: Author, Braider, Dancing, Leadership Coach, Notary Agent, Psychologist, Rapper, Tax Preparer, Truth Speaker, and Writer.

This is why it is important for you to identify your gifts and talents. They will get you through your journey of life. You will make some dumb decisions but learn from them. Learn from your mistakes. Do not repeat the same mistakes because that shows being stuck. Never repeat cycles. Later, it will all make sense as you grow and your mindset change.

Now my gifts and talents have grown into something special and successful. I can write poems, music and books. I love to dance. I am a Truth Speaker with a degree in Psychology. Remember I been finessing people before my time. I love getting into the minds of people. I love numbers so it was only right to get into

Taxes. I am the Queen of Plaits today (Addicted to Plaits). Everything I discovered as a child was all a part of my journey for my adult life I live today. Make your gifts and talents work for you, not work against you. I definitely made mine work for me.

CREDIT AND SAVING MONEY

I knew nothing about credit as a teenager. My mother was a Manager at a Finance company for many years. She taught me how to save money. But we never discussed credit. Until one day a friend of mine said we should apply for a Burdines card. I was like okay. I had no idea what I was doing. I did know my social security number. My mother made sure I learned that. I applied for my first credit card. The cashier showed me what to put on the application and everything. Then she said "Miss. Mchenry, you been approved for $500. You can use it today towards your purchase." I'm like hell yeah, run it!! I politely put my money back in my purse and signed the receipt. That was the beginning of building my credit. I started applying for every card there was. Now I am getting cards in the mail all the time. My mom started paying close attention. She was like what you are doing. I told her I was building my credit. That is what my friend said I was doing. My mom looked at me and said, you know you must pay these credit cards back? I said I know. I was not worried about that because I got so many hustles. Plus, I have a part-time job. I am good. Those credit card bills started rolling in back to back. I did not want to grow up in that way at all. I thought I did. So, I decided not to pay them after a few months. The biggest mistake I ever made. I started destroying my credit tremendously. I was still getting approved for things like phones and more store credit cards. So, I did not see no harm in what I was doing to myself. I thought I knew it all. If you think you know it all, stop thinking that way. Know it all people cannot be directed and guided correctly. They are not coachable. They do not take constructive criticism well. Do not be this type of person. You will not make it in the successful world. You will always remain average because you do not want to learn and listen.

By the time I got in my early 20s, my credit was shot. My mom tried to warn me. I just did not want to listen at the time. I knew I wanted a brand-new car and a place of my own. I had to find the credit repair guy immediately. We always want the quick way out. I want you to know that the quick way does not always be the right way. You get what you pay for. Pay your bills. Keep your credit good. Learn to save your money. Never be scared to invest into yourself.

The credit guy changed my entire world in a matter of time. I had money to pay the credit guy but would not use that same money to pay my bills. These are the dumb decisions I am talking about. I got my first apartment in my name. I brought my first brand new car in my name. And I got approved for a $8000 credit card. I went crazy. I am still making money every way I could. I was living my best life until the rent, car note, car insurance, light bill, cable bill, cell phone bill, started kicking in every 5 days. What the hell was I thinking? My money was starting to look funny because I was content with the hustling I did that accommodated my living arrangements at my parents' house. I forgot I was not living at home no more. I needed to increase my hustles. I need to go harder. It was time to step it up. Every hustle had to increase income. I had to re-evaluate from the hair prices to the dudes I was dealing with. Everything had to be stepped up a few notches. More clients, more money to flip more product, show money went up, hosting fees went up, no more dating the workers...my life required the Boss. I wanted the man that paid the workers. I had to step my game up all the way across the board. Are you still making the same amount of money from last year? If so, you need to re-evaluate your finances. The cost of living goes up every year. You cannot elevate if you are still in the same position of 6 months ago, a year ago. Lets step it up! Lets not be afraid of change. Step out on faith.

Good thing I learned how to budget and save my money. That knowledge took me a long way even till today. I will make a way out of no way. Do not live beyond your means. Know what you can afford. You are not here to impress the world. The world does not matter. When you are dead and gone, this world will keep going. The only thing you need to impress is God and the credit bureaus because nothing else matters. Do not live with Jones when you are an Allen. I know ladies who will buy a Gucci purse just to look like they got money. Do not be that lady. Do not buy a foreign car living in an apartment or staying with people. Please do not be offended. I speak off my opinions and my way of thinking. Live smart!

After realizing how my life shifted so fast because of the change of my living. I had to pump my brakes. I almost destroyed my credit again. I was determined to figure this adult life out the right way. All this time I did not have a bank account. I was a shoe box type of girl. I opened my first bank account at First Union before it became Wells Fargo. I always believed in the shoe box for many of years. It was time to grow up and save the right way. I did just that. I am now on the right track. My part-time job, my many gigs and a new dude in my life. I handled my business. He taught me so much. He even taught me things I had no business learning. I wanted all the game and the knowledge. Remember that people can take a lot of things from you but not your knowledge. Always educate yourself to be better. I never knew when I needed to use this game and knowledge later.

Today credit is important. Credit has always been important. Some of us just do not take it serious or did not take it serious. It takes discipline when you have good credit. It is easy to destroy and hard to piece it back together. If you have good credit, keep it that way. If your credit needs to be improved or fixed; do what needs to be done as soon as possible. Get your credit in order. You will need it. Credit is better than money. Street credit is only good in the streets. Street credit does not get recognized in the corporate world.

If you are a parent to a minor, start building their credit. Do not put lights in their name while they are children.

Do not destroy their credit before they could. Parents open them a bank account. Teach them how to budget, save, and spend. Teach them these fundamentals early because the schools do not teach our kids about life anymore. Kids need to learn this. The schools are not teaching our kids how to write in cursive. Many kids will grow up not knowing how to sign their name if they are not taught. Teach them to appreciate things of value. Dropping some gems on the parents who have minors. Stop teaching them that Jordans and Gucci is the way of life. We all want the best for our kids. But many people are teaching them to cherish material things. Many are teaching them that material things define who they are. It starts at home.

No matter how you make your money. Always pay yourself first. Take a certain amount of money and put it up. If it is hard for you to save. Open you a savings account. If you get direct deposit have a certain amount to go directly into your savings. Do not touch that money if you do not have to. If you do not have an account. Take a few dollars and go to the laundry matt. Put your money in the change machine. Take those coins and put them up in a jug. After a few months, cash in the change you saved. You will be amazed how much money you will have. It is important to know how to save your money. Make your money work for you. Everyone should have an emergency savings. Learn this early. Remember it is never too late to start. Saving was my number one advantage I had under my belt because I watched my mother. I love to see my money grow. If you do not need it; do not buy it! Wants and needs are two different things.

SET GOALS

I always had a master plan even if it was a dumb plan or smart plan. Either way it made money. I always thought ahead of the game. I set goals I wanted to achieve and the deadline I needed to achieve each one. I was always great at this. I love a challenge. I would always challenge myself for greatness. I still challenge myself every day. Challenges will strengthen who you are. Never be afraid to test yourself. Stop trying to piece things together in your head. This causes stress. Write everything down. You will feel better actually seeing your plan on paper. Try it!

Write out your goals and set a deadline for them. Be realistic. Do a 3-month goal setter. Do a 6-months goal setter. Do a 12-month goal setter. Write everything you will need to do to accomplish every goal you want to achieve. Whatever you set your mind to do, you can do it. Do not get thrown off your path of greatness. You must be determined and disciplined. Stick to your plans. If you come across a ditch, go around it and keep going. Stay focused! Remember it is never too late to start over. Only you know your life and the reality of it. If you want that car and you need to save money to get it. Evaluate your income. Determine what you need to make and how much you can afford to put up. Set your numbers based on your deadline.

You want to buy a car. How much is the car? How much do you make? How much you have saved? How much can you afford to pay a month? How much you want to put down as a down payment? How many paychecks or sells you need to make every day, every week, every month for the next 8 months? Do not create no situation that will cause you to stress and worry. Just be realistic. Every goal must have a plan. Strategy is key. Use the correct key to unlock your achievement. You can do it! Do not let anyone tell you, you cannot. Only you can stop you from achieving your goals. You are your worse enemy.

Write your goals:
_____

* _____

* _____

* _____

* _____

* _____

* _____

* _____

How long will it take you to achieve each goal?

* _____

* _____

* _____

* _____

* _____

* _____

* _____

How much money do you need to save every week?

* _____

* _____

* _____

*_____

Remember to be realistic. The key to success is eliminating stress. It is easier to see things better when they are written down. It is called a blueprint.

SPEAK LIFE INTO YOURSELF EVERYDAY

I realized one day that my tongue was a weapon. My tongue is extremely powerful. Your tongue is too. I learned that I needed to be very mindful of the things I said to myself and others. You need to be mindful of the things you say to yourself and others too. Always be stern with things of positivity. I was speaking more things of foolishness than I was of good at one point of my life. I would gossip about people for no reason. That type of behavior developed because of some people I chose to be around. It mainly was done with other females.

We as women will tare down another woman before we pick her up. We will believe a lie about someone but question the truth. We will gossip about people without knowing the full story. When will this stop? Do not be this person. Lift up your sisters in prayer. Empower and inspire another woman. Support their business. Build solid relationships with them. Stop thinking you better than others. Never be afraid to ask for advice or help.

I realized gossiping paid me no money and it did not pay my bills. This is also one reason I did not keep a gang of females around me. I realized I was sinning to the highest power. Every time I spoke bad against someone, I was delaying my blessings. I was also putting more energy into their blessings because I was discussing them in the wrong way. See God will show out for you in front of those who speak bad against you. I stopped all that gossiping and put that energy into something more productive. I changed the company I kept around me. Now me and my real friends discuss ways of getting money. We speak life into each other. We pray for each other and our business. We support each other. We celebrate each other accomplishments. We argue about who is going to pay the bill at the end of the night. As you mature, your mindset change. You no longer have the same taste for things you once craved for.

Every morning before I open my eyes, I thank God for blessing me with another unpromised day. I thank him for waking me up & confirming my job on earth is not finished. He gave me another chance to be better than I was yesterday. I am extremely thankful every day. I get up and speak life into myself and into my day. I tell the universe how my day will be. I empower myself with positive words of encouragement. I remind myself who I am. I tell myself I am beautiful. I tell myself I am a Queen. I tell myself I am a best-selling Author. I am wealthy. I speak these things into my life every day. I believe every word I say to myself and others. You must believe what you speak. It is easy to talk good but do you really mean it? Your heart must match your thoughts.

I listen to motivational speakers. I listen to Educators, Entrepreneurs, Positive Influencers, people of wisdom and knowledge. You must know how to reprogram your mind. Feed your soul with all great things. Always protect your peace at all times; by any means necessary.

Here are some of my favorite speakers:

- Les Brown
- Eric "ET" Thomas
- Joel Osteen
- Sarah Jakes

That is just to name a few…..

I want you to identify speakers who impact your life:

* _____

* _____

* _____

* _____

* _____

I just learned how to mediate. It was hard for me at first because I could not focus. I could not keep my mind from racing. I had to find peace within myself to be able to mediate correctly. Mediation puts you in a calm state of mind. It allows you to embrace positive frequencies from the universe. I always say be real with yourself. You will read that phrase a million times throughout this book. I say that all the time because it is easy to get lost in this world by distractions. You should find your happy space. What makes you feel good? What brings you peace? If you could live whatever life you desire right now, what would it be? Just make sure it is essential. What is stopping you from being happy? What is stopping you from living that life? What is blocking your happiness? What is interrupting your peace? Whatever it may be, disconnect from it. Remove it from your life. Your peace is your sanctuary. Your happiness is your life. If your life is not right, it is impossible to be happy. Speak life over all your situations. If your finances are not right; do not be a Debbie downer or a Depressed Denise. Speak life into your finances. The only way to have problems are having no solutions. Stop worrying! Stop stressing! Continue to pray. You must believe everything you speak. Please remember this. It is very important. You must have faith in everything you pray about. Always think positive to produce positive words to come off your tongue. It is never too late to start over and reprogram your mind.

Write down your own affirmations. Listen to other powerful people who speak affirmations. Speak those affirmations every morning as you look in the mirror. Say them with authority. Taste every letter of the word. And if you do not know what affirmations are; they are positive quotes to encourage, empower and inspire yourself and others. Eliminate conversations of distraction and no value.

Write down some affirmation you live by:

1. _____
2. _____
3. _____

4. _____

5. _____

Who can you influence?

1. _____
2. _____
3. _____
4. _____
5. _____

Always feed yourself knowledge!! And share with others.

MENTAL LOVE IS THE STRONGEST LOVE

Mental love is a beautiful thing if captivated correctly. This form of love must be experienced with yourself. You must know how to mentally love you before loving anyone else. Everything is ignited through the brain. To register anything in your head and act on it or speak it, you must have belief in it. Do you tell yourself "I Love You?" Do you hold your heart and tell it you are sorry for the pain and stress you have caused it? Tell your heart you love it because without it, you will not be alive. You must know how to mentally love yourself first.

Most of the time we think we are in love. Most of the time it is lust for the moment. Believing to be in love with the wrong things can throw you off your game plan. Believing you are in love could have you in messed up situations and far from being focused. Mentally loving yourself will protect you from settling for anything that does not deserve to share the same air as you.

I once loved a man who did not love me in return. He would tell me he loved me. But he would show me differently. He would buy me whatever my heart desired. He would give me the world. But he would cheat. He had no respect for me. I had to accept the truth and disconnect. I deserved better. I deserved so much more. I know my worth now. I will never settle for less than what I deserve. I do not need a man to define me. I need me to define who I am.

If they do not respect for themselves; how could they love you? Respect is the best love they can show you. When you are in love, you do not see nobody else. When another person can come into your relationship, being in love is out of the window. Both parties must respect each other. Pay attention to your spouse or companion. Pay attention to the picture they paint. Believe the artwork because paint cannot be erased.

I hear it all the time, I love them. Do they love you? Do they love themselves? How do they speak to you? How do they treat their mother? How do they take care of their kids? Do they motivate you to do better? Can they lead you? Can he lead you?

I speak on mental love because earlier I spoke about getting in the heads of guys. I learned how to manipulate guys in believing I liked them or loved them. I learned this before even thinking about going to college and studying Psychology. I already knew how to get in the mind of people. I just used my knowledge to my advantage. I became very observant to the way a guy talk, the way he walk, the type of clothes he wore, the way he acts, the friends he kept, the way he moves and the way he conduct business. Most of all the way he treated me. I would watch every detail until I found every loophole into a place where a piece was missing. If I knew he loved clothes; but he is always too busy to go to the mall. I would go and surprise him with a few outfits. Sometimes, I would have my boosters go to him and tell him to pick out some outfits. All paid for by me baby. If he was on the block all day. I would take him food to show him I cared or had it delivered to him and the boys. I would ask him certain questions like what he likes to do. If he seems too basic, I will introduce him to a life he never experienced. I would take a guy to a restaurant just to see if he knew how to sit at the table correctly. I wanted to see if he knew how to use a knife properly. I would always treat him like a King no matter what. Or put him in position to embrace the King in himself that he had no clue existed. I did this to get in his mental state of mind. Sometimes royal treatment can eliminate him from your world. Some dudes cannot handle being treated good. Once I know I have him in the palm of my hands, he will do everything necessary to keep me happy especially in the finance area. You never beg a man for money. If he loves you or feels he love you, he will do everything you need him to do without asking.

I hung around guys all the time. I learned a lot. I listened to my homeboys talk about what would get them to settle down or fall in love. I soaked up the game and mastered it. I had a lady tell me many years ago, "That cat between your legs is very powerful. If you know how to use it without giving it up, you can control the world." I wanted the world. You should want the world too.

When a person is mentally digging you or connected to you, they will do everything possible to keep you. My biggest mistake was dating dudes for the wrong reasons. I wanted him to match Pooh Gotti's fly. They did not know Lashonda because I was unfamiliar with her at the time. When I say the wrong guys, I mean all the ones I had no type of future with. Do not get it twisted, I really liked a few of them. The goal is to get him to love me and the rest is history. A man that loves a woman will make sure she is taken care of the best way he knows how to. I succeeded every time.

I am so in love with me now; mentally, physically, and spiritually. I mean every word I just stated. I am at a point in my life that I forget about dating sometimes. I am stress-free. I sleep great at night. I am not worrying about anyone cheating on me or using me. I am not afraid of giving the love I have to the right individual. Believe me, one day I will meet the man of my dreams. The man I pray for every day. The man God continues to mold me for every day. The man that will find me. Until then I am still working on me and accomplishing all my goals. Right now is not the time. The reason I know it is not the time because I have so much more to accomplish. I am too focused. I am not too blind to know when he shows up in my life. It is going to take a special type of man. I will not settle for less than I deserve.

Sis always work on loving you first. If you are in a relationship, still have time for yourself. Never forget to love who you are. Do not be that woman who get in a relationship and forget about her friends. Never do this. Never allow your spouse to make you do that. Never lose yourself in a relationship. You got this!! Mothers teach your kids self-love. Continuously tell them you love them. Teach them how to love themselves.

I was in a verbally abusive relationship one time. This relationship could have destroyed me. The love I genuinely had for this man blinded me to the mistreatment. I never had a man to hit me. I never experienced physical abuse. But verbal abuse can make you lose your mind. Verbal abuse can force you to always question yourself. Verbal abuse can send your entire self-esteem to zero. It was a good thing I knew better. It was a good thing I was mentally strong. I finally woke up one day and said I deserve much better. I walked away and never looked back. You know why I was able to walk away so easy? Not only did I know my worth; but it showed me how he treated his past relationships. I knew from that point I was better than the entire situation.

When you get into a new relationship, never think you are better than the ex. They are the ex for a reason. A reason you must learn for yourself. You must understand the individual you are in a relationship with. You may become the Ex also. Then you can understand why they cannot keep a relationship. I hate to hear about ladies feuding with each other because of a dude. Why? You cannot pawn his penis. It is not worth any value. I know love makes us do some crazy things. But fussing and fighting with another woman is not the answer. Be the bigger woman. It takes two to argue. Do not entertain anything that does not increase your bank account. Value yourself!! Know your worth!! Love yourself!!

I vowed to always build my daughter up. I will always tell her she is beautiful. I will always tell her how smart and intelligent she is. I will always support her. I do believe in being her friend but her mother first. Never lose the power of being their mother. I always wanted my daughter to be able to talk to me. I make sure I listen to her before reacting. Mothers keep a line of communication open with your children especially your daughters. I did not have a strong line of communication with my mother. This is why I did so much stuff in my early years.

Ladies understand your man or a man. Men are not taught to show their emotions. As kids they were always taught to be tough. They were taught that crying was for girls. Understand if a man talks and express himself, let him finish. It takes a real man to express himself verbally. We as women tend to always want to listen to respond. We sometimes need to listen to understand. Stop wanting to wear the pants, the tie, the shirt, and the skirt. You are the woman not the man. Let him lead. If he cannot lead you, he is not the man for you. You attract who you are.

Again, mental love must be established in your life so you can express and teach it to those you mentally love genuinely. Fall in love with yourself over and over again.

ESSENTIAL BUSINESS OWNER OR CORPORATE WORLD

Convid19 has been a life learned lesson for everyone. We experienced how the world can just stop at the blink of an eye. We experienced how our finances can be destroyed without warning. After experiencing this, it has forced me to rethink how I live my life from this point. I pray it you made you think the same thing. Any business I am a part of must be able to survive any situation such as Convid19. I plait hair. I became a Distributor for Total Life Changes for the 2nd time. I am an Author. I am a Leadership Coach. These are the things I did during this time to survive. The only business affected by this pandemic was my hair business because I could not do plaits. I practiced social distance completely. I refused to take chances with my health and my family. Money is not more important than my life and theirs. I focused all my energy into my books, into coaching others to success, and becoming a top seller in my network marketing company. I had more customers and enrollments during the pandemic than ever before. People brought more products to increase their immune system and improve their health. People joined the company because they saw I was still making money. They wanted a homebased business. They wanted to continue to have an income. I made more money during this time than when I first started. I released "Entangled Spirits: A Dangerous Game" on April 17, 2020. My book sells increased because everyone had time to read. Everyone wanted to feed their brain with knowledge. Reading is important for those who always want to enhance their life.

You must choose your investments wisely. Make sure your business can stand any pandemic. I know many business owners who suffered from this devastating situation. America never imagined anything like this ever. But now we know it is possible. Always be prepared and ready!! This will not be the first or the last. Making money on the internet is forever. Remember I think ahead of the game now. You should always think ahead too. Never get caught lacking anything. Have you a game plan because life is always changing. The world is always changing.

Those who have essential jobs. That is a blessing. I know many people who have essential jobs and go to work every day with the fear of catching a deadly virus. They are in fear of contacting anything that can harm them in any way. They are forced to go to work because they cannot afford to take off or lose their job. Many of them are not happy. You must ask yourself, is that what you want to do for the rest of your life. Is it worth it? These are questions to be answered.

Many of jobs will not be calling their employees back after they have laid them off. What would you do if you were in this position? Unemployment does not pay enough money to live off. If you do not have money saved, you going to stress and worry. Stressing and worrying enhance health issues. If you are not invested in your job, you have nothing. Even social security does not pay enough money to live off these days. I know many retired people who work part-time because the money is not enough.

Be your own boss. Make your own money. Call your own shots. I do not want to clock into nobody's job. I do not want nobody telling me when I can take off. Telling me when I can work. Telling me how much money I will make. I do not want someone to have the power of writing me up or firing me. I must be a business owner. That is my mindset. Everyone does not have that same mentality. Everyone not equipped to be a business owner and that is okay. But do not just be an employee. Get up the chart of chain of command and sit with the big dawgs. Be a part of those big meetings with the CEO and CFO. Get a position like that. Make working for someone worth it.

If you want a business, think about what kind of business you want. Again, think about what you are good at. Base your business venture on your gifts and talents. Loving what you do will never be considered work. It will be an enjoyment. Do not open a business because you feel it will make a lot of money or because others are making money from that type of business. What works for everybody may not work for you.

Again, open a business that is based on your gifts & talents. Your passion will attract the money.

If you can not cook, do not open a cooking business. If you do not know how to do hair, do not open a hair business. If you do not know anything about music, do not open a music company. You get my point. Open a business based off your abilities.

- What type of business you want?
- Name your business (choose 3 names just in case the first 2 not available)
- Incorporate you a business on Sunbiz.org
- Always have your paperwork in order

It is not hard to create a business. The hard part is keeping a business operating. Do you have the mindset to operate a business? You must be willing to market & promote your business 25/8. You must be willing to invest in your business. You must be sociable because you must network. You must build relationships with people. You must know how to talk to people. You must have great customer service. Every business owner does not have a business mentality. Please do not be that type of business owner. You will not last. You must know how to carry yourself professionally all the time. Remember, everyone is always watching you when you are popping.

BRAND AND MARKET YOURSELF

Energy! Energy! Energy! Your energy plays a vital role in your business. People are drawn in by your energy. They are drawn in by the life you show on social media and live outside of it. Always be mindful on what you post on your social media especially if you are a business owner. It is sad to say but people follow those who give them a perception of a life they desire. People follow people who has a large following. People follow those who will empower and inspire them. People follow those who provide great service.

Your profile picture should show your character. Your captions should capture your audience. Your bio should make them interested in knowing you. Your post should keep their attention. You must be active on all your social media platforms as a business owner or an influential woman. Never be afraid to interact with your audience. Every time you go live or post, you are entertaining them. Always put on a great show. They may not like or comment or share but they are watching.

Being a professional, it is important for you to be professional all the time. Never get out of character! Never allow people to make you react in a way that can cause damage to your image. People can be very mean and rude. Never allow comments of negativity throw you off your focus. This is just another form of tough skin. You must have tough skin for success. You must be able to take constructive criticism for success. Everyone will not like you. Everyone will not support you. You stay focused on your passion and everything else will fall in place.

You control your pages. You create the tone of who you are and what you want. Whatever position you hold, always keep it cute, mature, and professional. Again, promote yourself with class. People are watching you every time you go live, every time you hit load, and every time you step your foot out the door. They watch everything you say, you do, and you post. As soon as you do something out of character. You will know. The inboxes coming. The texts from long lost people are coming through. The comments are being made. Never give them the satisfaction to say anything negative. Do understand they will. You will have some people who comment negative things on a positive post just for attention. Do not entertain clowns.

The game of social media is to always be consistent. This is a rule in being a business owner. Remember never to entertain people or things that does not bring in money to your bank account. Wasted energy is wasted time. You cannot get it back. Make your every move your best move. Life is like chest. Move wisely then checkmate.

There are so many ways to promote yourself. Many platforms to engage with such as Facebook, Instagram, Twitter, Linkedin, TikTok, other groups that aligns with your business. Always find groups or pages that align with what you are involved with. Never let people talk you out of your dreams. They are your dreams. Achieve them!

Researching should be your best friend when you are serious about your life. You can never go wrong with knowledge. The more you educate yourself the powerful you become. Always educate yourself. I learned long time ago that your mind is dangerous when filled with knowledge. This is a reason I stayed on top of the game because I became fearless. I became untouchable. I became who God created me to be.

I started asking everyone for information. I am not afraid of the word NO. The word NO inspires me. It forces me to get on top of my business. I seek advice from those who have done what I am doing. I seek advice from those who have the reliable resources to get me in position of what I want. Everyone who was on the path I wanted to walk; I wanted to learn and still want to learn. I put that ego and pride to rest many years ago. I am never to prideful to ask for help. I will repeat that. I am not afraid to ask for help. Do not be afraid to ask for advice from someone that is a reliable source. I stated that previously. Great business owners know how to listen. This will take you far.

You are an Eagle. Do you know the facts of an Eagle? Let me school you on an Eagle:
- They represent Freedom and Power
- They are bold
- Their eyesight is amazing. They can spot a prey from miles away
- They fly high without worries

You are an Eagle. Embrace it!!

Everyone should be making money on their phones. Are you making money on your phone? Everyone should have some type of side hustle; if it is not full-time. One stream of income will never be enough. You will never get rich with the mindset of a 9 to 5.

Digital currency is the new era. You must conform to what is taking place right in front of us. The world is changing right before our eyes. You must learn to be very observant. Pay attention to everything. You do not have to be a Politician to know politics. Learn the game so you can stay in the game. I encourage you to educate yourself and research what our world leaders are talking about. Your future is in their hands. Learn how to play their game at your benefit. I google everything. I YouTube everything. It works! Make it work for you too.

PROTECT YOUR PEACE

Let me be real clear when I write this. Protect your peace by any means necessary. I do not care who it is. Let me repeat that. I do not care who it is. Disconnect from them immediately if they disturb your peace. I am protective of my peace. Once I experienced it for the first time, I always wanted it to stay that way.

Find you a peaceful place. My peaceful place is the beach. What is yours? I can go to the beach anytime of the day and enjoy every aspect of it. I love going out there because it is the place where all the energies meet. The water, the air, the sand, the water, the sun, the moon, the birds, the fish, etc.. everything connects at the beach. I love to listen the sound of the waves, the singing of the birds, and laughs of other people walking by or sitting near. I will close my eyes and relax. I embrace the environment with open arms. I mediate, pray, and write down my thoughts.

Find your peaceful place. Find you a place you can let down your hair and captivate your creativity. Having a PEACE of mind is better than a PIECE of mind.

List some places you can go to relax:

1. _____
2. _____
3. _____
4. _____

Whenever you feel discouraged or stressed, go to one of those places. Learn to refresh, regroup, and reset.

- Refresh- Take a deep breath. Start over on whatever it was you was going through. Dissect the situation and see what and where your situation went wrong
- Reset- Gather your thoughts. Listen to some motivational words. Listen to soothing music. If you are anything like me, sip on some wine. Stay in a happy place in your life. Always know how to get back to your happy place in life all the time
- Restart- Put your high positive energy back into the universe.

You do not always have to be going through anything wrong to go to your peaceful place. You can go there every chance you get. I enjoy going to my peaceful places even when I am being creative. I visit my peaceful places even when I am in a good space. I just love peace in my life. You should too. Find your peace and keep it!

WHO ARE YOU ALIGNED WITH?

I love to put myself around people of knowledge and wealth. I believe in rubbing shoulders with the people you are inspired by. I believe in manifestation strongly. I want you to learn to manifest everything you want. To manifest, you must believe in your thoughts. You must believe in your abilities to make it happen. You must believe in every word you speak into the universe.

You may think I am crazy. But these are some things I manifest in my life. I attend yacht shows because I manifest in owning one soon. I will rent a yacht for a few hours to enjoy the moment and manifest my ownership. I visit mansions because I will own one. I go to my rich friend's mansion because they can tell me how to get one. I go on the car lot of my dream cars and manifest in driving off the lot with the ones I desire. Speak it, think it, and it shall be yours! The powers are in your mind.

The people I am aligned with invite me places that many people wish they could go. I get invited to events that many wish they could be invited to. You can too. You can do any and everything you set your mind to. I visit homes of people that most of see on television. I say this because I align myself up with the right people to encourage me and bless me with knowledge to get the things I desire.

It is important to be aligned with the right people when you trying to be successful. It is important to get you a mentor or an accountability partner. I do not care how old you are, get a mentor. Get someone who you can be honest with and you can trust their advice. Try to align yourself with those who have more to offer you. They have more resources to give to you.

I am a tough friend. I am the honest friend. I do not care who you are. You must be able to feed my mind mentally. We must speak the same language. I am very intellectual. You must be able to match my energy. If not, we have nothing in common. I am not afraid to hurt my friends' feelings. I never do that in a mean way. I give tough love because I love hard. Either I deal with you or I do not. There is no grey area in my life. I have always been the strong friend. And when I am ready to be weak for a moment, I found myself not having that friend to lift me up. I got tired of that. So, I began taking my friends through bootcamp. After a few hard and honest talks, they either get mad and disconnect. Or they think about everything I said and come back for more. This is how you should view the people around you. Do not allow messy people in your space. Do not tolerate disrespect from anyone. You are the company you keep. My bootcamp is the process of elimination for my connection to you. I do not want nobody around me that is weak. We do not always have body weight to lose. Many of us need to lose deadweight of humans. Those people that bring no value to the relationship. You need to find new alignments if this is your connections.

I align myself with business owners. Why? Because I am a businesswoman. I align myself up with positive people. Why? Because I want my mind to only absorb positive things and stay within positive energy.

Align yourself up with homeowners. Why? Because they will teach you how to become one. If you already own a home or properties, teach others the knowledge you gained to become a homeowner. Align yourself up with people who is wealthy or making money. Why? Because they will teach you how to become wealthy and how to make money. Even when I am wealthy, I will continue to be around people with wealth because wealth has no cap on it. Numbers never stop calculating. So why should you? Stop putting limitations on your life.

I want you to list the type of people you want to align yourself with:

1. _____
2. _____
3. _____
4. _____
5. _____

Then I want you to list the type of people you are currently aligned with: (be honest)

1. _____
2. _____
3. _____
4. _____
5. _____

Are you proud of the list of people you currently aligned with? If yes, continue to manifest your life.
If no, it is time to disconnect and align yourself with people who can guide you to the things you desire in

your life. Being surrounded by the wrong energy will delay your blessings.

Lets get it! The world is yours…….There is no stopping you.

MAKE SMART INVESTMENTS

What is your income? Right now, how much money can you honestly say you have. Money that you can actually touch. Again, learn to save your money. Learn to pay yourself first then your bills. Designate a few dollars to put towards your "pay myself" savings.

I love residual income. Residual income is money that continuously reoccur. You want to always focus on residual income. I made many dumb investments. I was moving so fast and I wanted all fast turn arounds. Those are not always good. Good investments will bring you a great return. Good investments can set you up for a successful life.

I had a conversation with a guy one day. I will always remember what he told me. Invest in life insurance. He said a lot of people do not invest in life insurance because it seems to close to planning their funeral or planning the funeral of a loved one. The truth about life insurance is it can be beneficial to you. Do you know you can borrow from it? Having life insurance is important. It not only take the cost of burial expenses but it can set you or your family for financial freedom. I immediately purchased life insurance policies on everyone in my household. I want my daughter to be financially set when I pass away. I want her to have a business mind and invest her money to see more money. I am thinking ahead of the game. Time waits on nobody.

I never understood how dudes could be in the streets making so much money but when they die, the family selling dinners or raising money. It is not just guys. It is people in general. Save your money! Invest it into something that will benefit you and your family.

Invest into your business. Do not be afraid to put money into yourself. If you do not feed your business, how you expect other people to feed it. Invest your money into things that hold value.

- Purchase jewelry (real jewelry)
  - Pawn or Sell
- Purchase shoes (real shoes)
  - Sell later to someone, on Ebay, etc.
- Purchase purses (no knock offs)
  - Sell later to someone, on Ebay, etc.

We all love to look good. I never was the type of woman stuck on name brands. I knew females who would buy Gucci, Fendi, Chanel, etc.. and do not have no money in their purse. They would have a $1000 purse with $5 in it and -$100 in the bank. I will never carry a purse that cost more than what I have in my bank account. You not trying to impress the world. You want to take care of you and your family. I do not knock nobody lifestyle. I am speaking from my own point of view. I do not believe in driving a fancy car and living in the projects. I want to own a home and have a fancy car in my driveway or garage. Some things do not make sense to me. But that is my opinion. This is how I view my life. This is the order of my life. What is the order of your life? What makes sense to you?

If you have a fancy car and you stay in the projects, please invest into a home. Purchasing a home is a great investment. You can build equity in your home. It will allow you to borrow money from your home. Make all your money make sense. And make it work in your favor.

Money is not the only thing that relates to investments. Your time is an investment. You can not get your time back. Do not waste your time on people or things that is not worth it. Relationships are investments. We all have made bad investments in this area some point in our life. I do not cherish nothing I cannot pawn especially when it comes to a man.

Many years ago, my mother had a friend who was at our house. Her and my mother was having a grown folk conversation. But I could hear them talking. She was telling my mother about this man she was dating. They had a big argument and the guy told her to give him back everything he brought her. Her response to him will forever stick in my head. She said, "When you can give me back my vagina (not that word) I will give you back your stuff." So, if he can not give you back that, you do not give him back nothing. I lived by that all my life. Once you give it to me it is mine.

How much money you want to make every week? How much money you need to make a day for 5 days? Lets say you want to make to $1000 a week. You will need to make $200 a day. How can you make that? Think of ways to get you to your goal. There are so many ways to make $200 a day.

What you like doing? What are you passionate about? How many people you need to purchase your product or service at your set price?

Example: I plait hair. I charge $250 (small plaits). I need one head per day.

- Follow my IG: @Lashonda_World & @Addicted_to_plaits
- To book: Letstalkbusiness2004@gmail.com

Invest into yourself!!! Scared money never makes money. I will always encourage people to be risk takers.

I will always encourage people to be business owners. Make your own money and be your own boss.

Invest into seminars and workshops. Invest into classes that will further your business or career. Try to attend as many networking events or social gatherings as possible. Do not be afraid to put yourself in the mist of people of your desires. If you love to paint. Attend local art shows. If you love doing hair. Attend that hair shows. What ever you love doing, attend every event you come across to further your dream and align yourself up with people in the same field. Follow people who share the same passions and desires as you on social media. Do not be afraid to inbox or DM people to connect with.

Invest into yourself!!!! You can do it. Lets get connected.

PASSION ATTRACTS BLESSINGS AND MONEY

By now you should know what you love to do. You should be prepared to take over the world. Your passion will always be a magnet to your blessings and money. You must stay consistent. You must have great customer service. You must have a pleasant attitude. Remember you need product or a service to give your consumers. Customers will later become clients. Always keep your clients informed. They love being updated on everything. Communication is key. Understanding is power.

Never knock other people hustle. We mind only the business that pays us. Keep your heart good. God judge us by our heart not our actions. One ounce of envy & jealousy for someone else, will put you in the losing seat.

If you have broken relationships with anyone. Please find a way to mend them. We can not ask for blessings with a harden heart. This can hinder your blessings and delay your financial blessings.

The only person you are competing with is the person in the mirror. You must stay focused on the prize. If everyone is busy making money; many people would not have time for foolishness. Idle time can create a negative energy and environment in some people. Overthinkers tend to overdose on thoughts of negative. Please do not overthink nothing. Quarantining during the pandemic exposed a lot of people and their mindset. This situation should have made you a better person. It should have forced you to think outside of the box that you may stay locked up in. You should know how to handle this every time it occurs in the future.

Stay prayed up and build your relationship with God. I am blessed because of my relationship I built with God. I talk to him like he is right next to me. I seek him for everything I need in my life. I was not always like that. At one point in my life during my Pooh Gotti days, I thought I knew it all. I thought I knew it all. It almost costed me my life. I will never try to control my own life ever again. God will always lead me. I will always follow.

Again, my heart is pure. I released all ungodly feelings towards everyone I had a problem with. I released all that negative energy to make room for all the positive energy.

Allow your work to show for you. Your work will reveal your passion. You must love what you do.

Remember I am self-employed. I will always encourage others to work for themselves. Do not get me wrong. I love hard working people in the workforce. Am not one of those people. I use to be. Then I realized I do not like following directives. I needed to put my passion on the frontline and step out on faith. I did that. So, I promote being a business ownership.

My biggest enjoyment is writing this book and sharing all these positive nuggets with you. I want every woman to win. I want every woman to know who she is and her purpose for life. Be a powerful impact on other women. Let the knowledge you possess, educate and motivate other women. Let your passion be the healing for another woman who can not find her way. I share these words for you to share with other women. When your heart is good, it will open multiple doors that your hustle can not open. It is favor from the most high. Let your success speak for you. You do not have to speak a word out of your mouth. The best revenge is success.

Continue to feed your mind positive words. Continue to be around positive people. Continue to follow your purpose by knowing your passion. Continue embracing your peace. Continue to stay focused. Continue to help others. Helping others will bring you so many blessings. Help others and do it with no expectations. Do it from the pureness of your heart. You will continuously be blessed and forever be a blessing. Until you meet someone name "They"; you should not let "They" disturb your mission or care what "They" say.

DEFEAT THE ODDS

Stop using your past as an excuse. Embrace your past and forgive yourself. We all have a story. Some will tell their story and some will not. Those that choose not to share their stories are not fulfilling their calling. They afraid to be talked about. They are ashame to be embarrassed to themselves and others. Self-check yourself all the time. We are not put on this Earth to judge nobody. That is not our job. Stop judging people. Do your opinions pay her bills? Do their opinions pay your bills? Do not let the world dictate your greatness. You tell your story. I challenge you to be a blessing with your story. Your story can touch the life of another woman. Be that impact on another beautiful woman. Tell your story to the world. Allow God to use you in an amazing way. Your story could help millions of ladies. Be the reason she broke her silence and moved forward.

Feeling embarrassed and shamed is the spirit of the enemy. I never been embarrassed or shame of my past. I will tell anyone my story. I use to cry about not being further in life because of choices I made. But I was never shame of things I did. My experiences made me the woman I am today. I am a winner. I cannot be defeated. I beat the odds. And you can too.

What are some things you need to overcome to allow you to elevate to your next level?

* _____
* _____
* _____
* _____
* _____

If you are a woman who is afraid to open up and tell your story, ask God to take those spirits of embarrassment and shame from you. God does not give us those feelings. He wants us to share our stories because it glorifies him. Do you notice I use the word "NEVER" a lot? I use that word because it is a word of strength and power. People say never say never. I will forever say never because I mean every letter. And everything is "YOU CAN" never say you cannot.

I can achieve everything I put my mind to. You must believe that also. No matter what you been through. The blessing is you made it through. Now keep pushing!! Make God proud. Make yourself proud. Make your kids proud. Make your family proud. Break generational curses. Be the first to own a successful business in your family. Make it happen! Change lives one day at a time.

Look up to the sky. Do you see a ceiling or roof beyond those clouds? Why do you question your ability to be great? Step out on faith and TKO that spirit of defeat and fear. We are unstoppable. You must believe that. You are victorious.

Take a piece of paper and write a letter to yourself. I want you to apologize to yourself for holding yourself back. After you write it, please read it. Once you read it and really feel what you wrote. Take that letter and tare it in small pieces. Go to the beach and release it into the ocean. Take it set it on fire. Let those words become pieces of your past. Let it go!! Now every time you speak your story, it will be to share with the world. It will be to help others. You will now smile as you tell your story. Your tears will be of happiness. First let your story inspire you.

I want it all. You want it all. We are going to get it. There is nothing to stop me but me. We can be our biggest enemy. Get out of your own way. You know everyone does not want to see you win. They have no power over your life. Only your belief in their energy can disturb your vision. If you believe people have power over you; they do because you believe they do. You know the saying do not fight fire with fire. That is a true statement. It goes for negative with negative. It goes for evil with evil. When people wish bad against you. You keep your focus on the bigger picture. Let God deal with them.

SECURE THE VAULT

You want to be the BAG. You also want to the woman who secure the vault that protects the bags. You are the bag!! You are a Boss. You call your own shots. You make your own money. Time to mentally understand your position. You are on a different level. I love mental clarity because reprogramming the mind is phenomenal. Sis are ready to secure the vault? If so, you should be able to answer these questions below.

- Did you discover who you are?
    - Who are you?
- Did you identify your gifts and talents?
    - What are they?

- Do understand the importance of credit? Do you understand the importance of saving money?
  - What is your credit score?
- Did you set your goals?
  - What are your goals?
- Do you speak life into yourself?
  - What are your affirmations to yourself?
- Do you understand mental love?
  - Do you love yourself? How do you express this type of love?
- Are you essential?
  - How?
- Do you know how to brand and market yourself and your business?
  - How?
- Will you protect your peace?
  - By what means?

- Are you aligned with the right people?
  - Who?
- Have made any investments? Do you plan to make investments?
  - What type of investments?
- Do you know how to use your passions to receive your blessings and financial abundance?
  - How?
- Have you embraced your past? Have you forgiven yourself? Will you use your story to help others?
  - How will you defeat the odds?
- Are you ready to secure the vault?
  - Are you capable of being a boss in charge of your life? Remember God first!
  - Are you ready to be the bag and represent yourself on that level? How?

I am so proud of you. You are on your way to success. You must stay determined and focused. Never take your foot off their neck. First take your foot off your own neck. We will use the heads of those who do not believe in us as stepping stones. Take every lesson learned as another certification under your belt. Never look back! Whatever is behind you, is behind you. Keep it behind you. You must leave it there.

We are stepping into another level of life every day. A life that will not allow everyone to be accepted. You must know your worth. You must hold yourself on a high pedal stool. Never downplay your standards to accommodate a person who do not meet your requirements. Your energy will attract everyone and everything aligned with you. We are who we attract. Let that marinate!

HIGH FREQUENCY OF ENERGY: LAW OF ATTRACTION

This may be the final chapter of this book; it is the beginning of your new life. How you see yourself? Your energy is transferred into the universe every day. Starting with how you wake up in the morning to start your day. Every day be thankful for waking up. Do not pick up your phone soon as you open your eyes. Do not open your eyes before giving him thanks and saying your prayers.

Let me tell you how my mornings go faithfully.

I wake up. I thank Him before I even open my eyes. I say my prayers. When I open my eyes, I grab my bottle of water and drink. I keep a bottle of water next to my bed for that purpose. Once I drink my water. I grab my phone but still not looking through it to see a missed call or unread text messages. I do not check my social media until later. I walk to the foot of my bed. Then I stretch. I sit down in Indian style. I use my phone for music to motivate me. Then I mediate for 10 minutes. When I go to the bathroom, I look in the mirror and began to speak life into myself. I look myself directly in the eyes and speak life into me.

I want you to speak life into yourself every day. Motivate yourself with words of encouragement. Compliment yourself! Speak confidence! Speak Life! Always speak life into yourself and others.

Energy! Energy! Energy! Energy attracts the world around you. Energy controls everything in the universe. Place yourself on a high frequency of energy. First you must believe to embrace your powers. You must believe you are beautiful to embrace your beauty. You must believe you are rich to embrace your wealth. You must believe you are strong to embrace your strength. You must believe you are a winner to embrace your victories. Your thoughts will manifest everything you believe. Everything starts in the mind. Your mind is powerful. That is why the enemy wants it so bad. Do not let him have it. Do not let that happen. Keep your frequency level of positivity high. You will see the difference of how your life change. You will see how people accept you. Remember you must believe in yourself. You must know you can do all things. When you feel defeated… refresh, reset, and restart.

Again, Thank you!! You are the BAG…

I pray you take my words and apply them to your life forever. Share this book with every woman you know. They must get their own copy because they must go through the Academy also. Recommend this book to other women you feel need this encouragement.

I am proud to announce that you have officially passed this course. You have graduated with high expectations of producing a life bigger than you ever imagined. Your new mindset now begins.

As of today, you are officially "The BAG!" Congratulations!!!

Much Love,

Coach Shon

Thank you so much for supporting me.
It means the world to me. We must always build each other up. Never again will we speak against another sister. We will not tare each other down. Lets show love to one another and support each other. We all we got!! And it starts with you.
Let's connect sis!

Sis, you are the **BAG!**

www.ingramcontent.com/pod-product-compliance
Lightning Source LLC
Chambersburg PA
CBHW071420210526
45465CB00001B/466